D1275787

Lay, R.
A green kid's guide to soil
preparation.

A Green Kid's Guide to
Gardening!

A Green Kid's Guide to Soil Preparation

by Richard Lay
illustrated by Laura Zarrin

magic
wagon

visit us at
www.abdopublishing.com

Looking Glass Library™ is a trademark and logo of Magic Wagon.

Printed in the United States of America, North Mankato, MN.
102012
012013

 This book contains at least 10% recycled materials.

Text by Richard Lay
Illustrations by Laura Zarrin
Edited by Stephanie Hedlund and Rochelle Baltzer
Interior layout and design by Renée LaViolette
Cover design by Renée LaViolette

Library of Congress Cataloging-in-Publication Data
Lay, Richard.
  A green kid's guide to soil preparation / by Richard Lay ; illustrated by Laura Zarrin.
       p. cm. -- (A green kid's guide to gardening!)
   ISBN 978-1-61641-947-9
1. Gardening--Juvenile literature. 2. Beds (Gardens)--Juvenile literature. I. Zarrinnaal, Laura Nienhaus. II. Title. III. Series: Lay, Richard. Green kid's guide to gardening!
   SB457.L39 2013
   635--dc23
                              2012023793

Table of Contents

Green Gardeners

Have you heard about "being green" at school or on television? It might sound like that means only wearing green clothes or eating green food. But, "being green" means learning how to live on Earth without hurting it.

A person who grows vegetables, fruit, or flowers is a gardener. People can be green gardeners. They can grow plants and protect Earth at the same time. With a little help from an adult, you can be a green gardener.

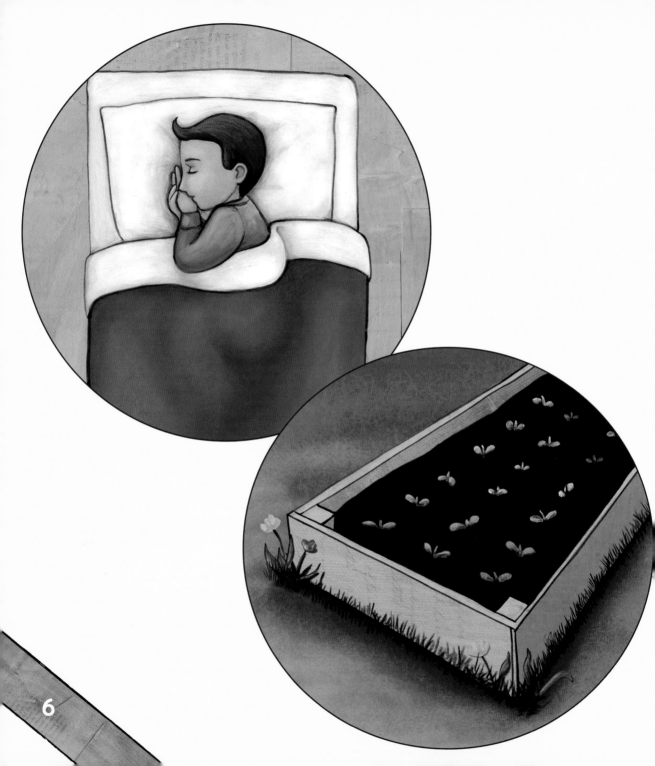

Raised Beds

A green gardener understands that plants are like people. A person needs a good bed to get sleep and grow strong. A plant needs a good bed, too.

Plants need a raised bed in order to be healthy and grow strong. A raised bed is a place where the soil is higher than the ground around it. Just like your bed, a raised bed has a frame, a mattress, and blankets.

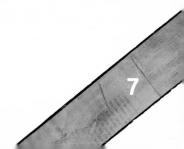

Select a Site

Not every place in your yard or school ground is good for growing plants. You need to look around for the best place to make your bed.

First, look up. Do you see trees and shade? If so, that would not be a good place to build your raised bed. Most plants need many hours of light every day to grow. So, pick a place with a lot of sunlight.

Next, look for a flat area. Would you like to sleep on a bed that leans to one side? You would roll off every night. A raised bed needs to be flat. Level or flat ground helps keep water in the soil.

Next, see if there is water nearby. Like you, plants need a lot of water to grow. You need a faucet and a water hose nearby. It will make watering your plants easier than carrying watering cans.

Finally, look down. Ask an adult to find out where pipes and wires are buried. The companies that put them there will be happy to help. You do not want to dig and cut a wire.

How Big of a Bed?

Like your bed at home, your raised bed garden needs a frame. You have picked a place to put your raised bed. The next step is to decide how big it should be. Kneel down and reach across the site.

How far you can reach is how wide your raised bed should be. You should not walk on your raised bed. If you walk on it, you push the soil down and take out the air. It also hurts the roots of your plants. So, you can only work in your raised bed as far as you can reach while kneeling.

Measure Your Site

Now you have a site. You also know how wide the bed can be. It is time to measure out your bed. The first step is to decide the length of your bed. You can cut the boards to fit the size of your bed, but 12 feet (4 m) long is a good size.

Next, place small sticks at each corner. Then run string from corner to corner. Now you know how big your raised bed will be. Use the string as a guide for digging. Dig holes along the string about 2 to 3 inches (5 to 8 cm) deep. Now you are ready to put the frame together.

Build the Frame

With an adult's help, go buy your wood. Try to buy wood that is not pretreated. The toxic chemicals in pretreated wood can hurt your soil, your plants, and you. Cedar wood that is not pretreated will last for many years.

With an adult's help, cut the wood. Make sure it is the size you need for your raised bed. Then, using "L" brackets and screws, join the four pieces of wood together. Now you are ready to put your frame on your site.

Prepare the Soil

You have put your frame in place. Now you must remove all of the grass. With an adult, use a hoe to dig up the grass. Put this grass in your compost pile. Then loosen the soil with a pitchfork.

Now, build your mattress in layers. Put a layer of newspaper in the frame. Then sprinkle a mixture of molasses and water on top. Use one tablespoon of molasses for every quart of water. This will bring in worms.

Next, put down a layer of organic materials. Do not use chemical fertilizers. Your final layer will be several inches of topsoil. Then cover all of it with a black plastic sheet. Let your raised bed sit for one or two months.

Get a Blanket

Before you can put seeds in the ground, you must make blankets for your raised bed. Remove the plastic and turn the soil over with a pitchfork. Do this one small square of soil at a time.

After turning over the soil, add a layer of compost or cow manure. On top of this add chopped-up leaves or grass clippings. Then add more compost. Now your raised bed has several layers of food for your plants.

You know that you need a frame, good soil, and several blankets. You don't use herbicides or chemical fertilizers. You can grow plants with organic things like compost, cow manure, grass, and leaves. You are ready to be a green gardener and plant your seeds!

A Container Garden

You will need:
Topsoil
Compost
A five-gallon plastic plant container
A packet of pepper seeds

1. Mix the topsoil and compost together and pour it into the plastic container and water the mixture.
2. Plant four or five seeds several inches apart. Push each seed down about one inch (3 cm). Place your container in a window that gets sunlight for several hours a day.
3. Keep a diary of what happens in your container garden each day:
     a. the day you plant
     b. each day you water
     c. the day you see sprouts
     d. the height of your plants
     e. the number of flowers
     g. when you harvest
4. Enjoy your peppers.

Glossary

compost: decaying things that were once alive. It is used to make soil healthy.

fertilizer: chemicals put into or on top of soil to make plants grow.

herbicides: chemicals used to kill plants.

manure: the waste of animals or livestock that can be used to fertilize land.

organic: of, using, or grown without chemical fertilizers or insecticides.

pretreat: to put chemicals into something to make it last a long time.

toxic chemicals: substances that can hurt a person.

Web Sites

To learn more about green gardening, visit ABDO Group online. Web sites about green gardening are featured on our Book Links page. These links are routinely monitored and updated to provide the most current information available.

www.abdopublishing.com

Index